INTRODUCTION

Everyone who was a child back in the 1950s or '60s will remember the long, hot summer holidays that seemed as though they would never end. For the fortunate there was a week's holiday at the coast or in the country, maybe even a fortnight if you were really 'well to do'. The less-affluent may just have had to make do with a day excursion, like my family's rare coach trips to Belle Vue Zoo. Whatever the case, the anticipation of the trip and the actual journey was usually just as important.

Package holidays and air flights abroad at that time were unknown and holidays were almost entirely taken in Britain, mainly by rail. However, as Dr Beeching's Axe began to swing on the railways, many seaside lines and country branches were rapidly closed.Thereafter, the mode of transport changed from rails to roads and as private car-ownership was still a long way from becoming widespread, motor buses became the order of the day. Yet, as the majority of the British coaches were in the 29 to 35-seat range in the 1950s, it was obvious that trends would have to change for the following decade.

Above: *Three firms were offered research chassis by Bedford, these being Duple, Plaxton and Weymann. However, so secret was this deal, that there is no date shown for these trials in the records. This Plaxton VAL is built on research chassis RHD62/1, and it carries Bedfordshire plates (477 CTM), which date from late-1960.* Vauxhall Motors

The biggest change came in 1961 when the regulations for chassis changed from a maximum 30' to 36' (11-metres), whilst the width went to 8' $2^{1}/_{2}$". Firms like AEC and Leyland were able to extend their existing Reliance and Leopard chassis, but the smaller chassis makers could not. They therefore had to come up with a larger capacity model, and at the same time keep a relatively lower price than the high class chassis. To meet this challenge, Bedford introduced their new VAL, which had the capacity for up to 52-seats. The new innovative coach quickly came to be utilised by a lot of the major luxury touring coach businesses and many of the minor ones too!

Robert Berry   Penrith, August 2007

3

THE VAL HISTORY

To understand the history of the Bedford VAL, the reader really needs to consider Volumes One, Two and Four in the *Fare Stage* series, as these explain how Vauxhall Motors' bus range developed from the Chevrolet chassis that were imported to Britain from the end of World War I onwards.

There were several significant steps in the development, most notably with the OB chassis that was introduced in 1939, just before the outbreak of World War II. There is no denying that the OB became one, the best-known of all Bedford PSV chassis.

The outbreak of war saw production halted, but a wartime OWB version, substantially contributed to the welfare of the country in a time of crisis. It was the only authorised British single-deck bus to be produced during the war, and despite its utilitarian accompaniments, it served in hundreds of fleets that would never have previously considered a Bedford chassis.

Above: *The Bedford VAL model made its debut at the Earls Court Commercial Motor Show in 1962, including this white painted chassis No.1000. The VAL employed many components from the Bedford TK truck range to reduce costs, a fact that was displayed on this chassis wherever it was subsequently put on display.* Vauxhall Motors

The dependability and economic operation of the Bedford bus/coach chassis won-over many new owners to the Marque, and many of these stayed loyal to the subsequent post-war OBs and the later models. Then, during the early 1950s, came the permitted extension of chassis to a length of 30' and 8' wide.

This in turn allowed greater seating capacity, but the larger chassis still tended to employ half-cab bodies, with the driver not only way in front of the passengers, but often having a bulkhead in between them. This also prevented easy one-man-operation, when the buses were used on fare-stage services.

Fare Stage
Volume Six

THE
BEDFORD VAL

Robert W. Berry

Nostalgia Road Publications

CONTENTS

The **Nostalgia Road** Series ™

is produced under license by

Nostalgia Road Publications Ltd.
Units 5 - 8, Chancel Place, Shap Road Industrial Estate,
Kendal, Cumbria, LA9 6NZ
Tel. +44 (0)1539 738832 - Fax: +44 (0)1539 730075

designed and published by
Trans-Pennine Publishing Ltd.
PO Box 10, Appleby-in-Westmorland, Cumbria, CA16 6FA
Tel. +44 (0)17683 51053 Fax. +44 (0)17683 53558
e-mail: admin@transpenninepublishing.co.uk

and printed by
Kent Valley Colour Printers Ltd.
Kendal, Cumbria - +44 (0)1539 741344

© Text: Trans-Pennine Publishing Ltd. 2007
© Photographs: Author's collection or as credited

Front Cover: *New to Heaps of Leeds, Harrington-boddied CNW 155C passed to John Hood before being withdrawn and allowed to decay. Purchased by Trans-Pennine for preservation, before Kenzies of Spereth superbly restorated it. Martin Kenzie*

Rear Cover Top: *Epitomising the early VAL14 models fitted with the Duple Vega Major body, 44 EMO was new to Eagle Line of Swindon. This one featured a very early chassis - namely 1025, and was thus in the first ten production sales models to be produced after the 15 demonstrators (1001-1016).*

Rear Cover Bottom: *Parked in an isolated back-street awaiting further duties with Watsons is DJH 749G one of a brace of VAL70 coaches that were new to Essex Coaches in 1969.*

Title Page: *Patrons of William Moxon's tours enjoy the tranquillity of the environs of the Peak District's Upper Derwent Valley on board 375 RVO, a Plaxton-bodied VAL14 of 1963. Vauxhall Motors*

This Page: *Undoubtedly a very rare photograph, this shows the first VAL14 chassis RHD60/1 during its first outing on the Vauxhall Text Track in 1960. It clearly shows the twin axle arrangement and the position of the engine. Interestingly, it was originally intended to use a Bedford petrol power unit. Vauxhall Motors*

ISBN 978 1903016 73 2
British Cataloguing in Publication Data
A catalogue record for this book is available from the British Library

The introduction of the underfloor engine chassis and the fitting of full-front bodywork on coaches, dated the traditional front engine half-cab vehicles almost overnight. Commer had appreciated the demand was about to change and they consequently developed the Commer Avenger in 1948. This was Bedford's big rival, and whilst the 29-seat OB was still selling like 'hot cakes', Luton countered with their 33-seat SB 'Big Bedford' in 1950, which was a derivative of the S-Type truck range. Whilst lower in height, than their trucks, the SB bus only achieved its low floor by using a chassis that curved upwards over the rear axle. Yet, it was well known by Bedford's engineers, but never admitted, that this was a potentially disastrous weak point in the design. Indeed, some serious fractures on early chassis were only rectified at great expense until efforts were made to obtain better quality steel, which was employed from 1956 onwards, but the design engineers kept advocating the necessity of having a straight and level floor.

In a 1956 development with their wheel and tyre suppliers, Bedford built an experimental truck chassis on 18" wheels, and towards the end of 1957 the wheels were lowered further to 16". The full details concerning the experiment have not survived in the Vauxhall records, but it would appear from those involved that extensive testing was done during 1957-8.

The test unit was a 29' two-axle 'road-legal' box van on 16" wheels, which was heavily disguised to conceal its true identity. Test driver, David Sayer recalls that, "in 1959 two longer chassis were introduced for clandestine testing in Europe." Both of these were fitted with a Primrose second axle, with one chassis having this axle at the front and the other at the back; the two configurations were done to test weight-carrying capacity for both truck and PSV use. A demonstrator model of the back-axle truck is shown in the picture at the top of page four, where a ten-ton TK is seen in the Research & Development area.

Top Right: *Three more test chassis (RHD62/1-3) were built in 1960-1 and these were allocated to various body builders in early 1962. One of these (RHD62/2) is seen undergoing the obligatory tilt-test in late-March 1962.* Vauxhall Motors

Bottom Right: *In May, the same Duple Vega Major-bodied coach (registered 825 CYR), climbs a slope on the Chobham test ground. This chassis was never sold into the PSV market, but was retained for use as a mobile test bed. An observation coach body was fitted to it in mid-1963, and a picture of this is seen on page 46 of* Bedford Buses of the 1950s & '60s, *but this body style was never put into production.* Vauxhall Motors

The VAL 14

Although most of the UK bus builders had begun increasing the seating capacity on a variety of chassis, it still took one-and-a-half to two coaches to replace the seating capacity of a standard railway carriage. Considering excursion trains of those days carried anything up to 14 carriages, 21 motor coaches were needed to replace one train. Indeed, cynics will say that the government's permission of new 10m chassis was a sop to allow the widespread railway closures that were being planned.

Prior to the new legislation, high-capacity buses, such as the original AEC Renown and the Leyland Titanic were built on a three-axle chassis. Three-axle single-deckers had also been manufactured too, such as the many AEC examples of London Transport. Trolleybuses had also long been built on three-axle chassis, but invariably all these PSVs had their twin axles at the rear rather than at the front. So, whilst AEC, Daimler and Leyland, offered their customers versions of their established underfloor engine models on extended chassis; Bedford on the other hand designed a completely new chassis.

Above: *This export body on a left-hand-drive VAL14 is quite a mystery. Differing suggestions have been made about the make of body, including MCW and Willowbrook, but neither of these seem correct. We are sure that this is chassis No.1014, but why did Vauxhall retain this picture in their file of VAL prototype pictures?* Vauxhall Motors

Bedford's approach to supplying a higher capacity vehicle chassis was decidedly different and quite unorthodox; yet it was fundamentally logical too! Rather than extending the SB chassis, which would have presented substantial engineering problems, the new low-height/level floor chassis was taken through development to a finished product. As a result, the VAL was their first PSV chassis not to be developed from a truck range, although it did embody many components from the new Bedford TK range, which in turn used several parts from the TJ series introduced in 1958. This served to keep the price down, both through the use of proven products (and hence no major development costs) and also from the benefits that could be obtained through mass production!

The trials of the three-axle experimental 'truck' were so successful, that in 1960 a prototype RHD60/1 'Chinese Six' chassis was built, with twin-steering front axles. The frames were designed and built from 'channel-section' side-members, which swept downward and inwards to give a low-level entrance. It had a wheelbase of 19' 3", and this allowed vehicles to be constructed to the new overall maximum length of 36'.

The VAL had a six-cylinder Leyland 0.400, 131bhp direct-injection diesel engine of 6.54-litres capacity, which was mounted vertically at the front of the chassis. The drive was taken through a Clark five-speed synchromesh gearbox (built under license by Turner) via a 14" dry plate clutch. This system gave a five-speed gearbox with direct drive to fourth and an 'overdrive' top speed. The 16" diameter wheels were the same size as used on the two-ton Bedford TJ2, as opposed to the normal 20" wheels used on other comparable PSVs. This in turn allowed for softer suspension and a smoother ride.

When bodied, the VAL had an unladen weight of between six-tons ten-cwt and seven-tons ten-cwt; the variation obviously being dependant on the coachwork fitted. The combination of the small wheels and the lower floor height enabled a reduction in the overall weight of the vehicle by almost one-ton. The new VAL14 made its debut in August 1962, and the chassis illustrated on page four was exhibited at the Commercial Motor show that year, along with fully finished examples by Duple and Plaxton. Bedford were able to offer the new chassis at a price of £1,775, which was rather remarkable as it offered a saving of almost £1,000 against the underfloor engine chassis that were being marketed by their competitors.

Top Right: *Blackpool was the venue of this crowded scene, as 1963 VAL (293 LG), a Plaxton-bodied coach from Lofthouse of Mickle Trafford, takes part in the driving test at the Northern Coach Rally that same year.*

Middle Right: *Demonstrator chassis 1007 had the first style of the Vega Major body with a rather fussy side flash towards the rear. As 5399 TF it later joined the fleet of Bold of Melling, and is seen here heading for Skipton in the Yorkshire Dales.*

Bottom Right: *Showing the contrast between the half-cab coaches of the 1950s and the VAL of the 1960s, we visit Wilson of Whitburn, who were one of two companies that traded under the fleet name of Economic. They bought this Duple Vega Major VAL14 (FPT 440C) in January 1965, which is seen next to an Albion with bodywork by ACB of Sunderland.*

THE VAL BODY BUILDERS

The VAL serial numbers began with No.1000, and this one was retained un-bodied as a display unit. There were then 15 'builder sample' chassis (1001-15), and these were tentatively allocated just after the 1960 Commercial Motor Show. Of these, Duple were to get seven (1001-3, 5-8), one of which was to be bodied as a service bus. Plaxton were allocated 1004 and 1009. The following firms would get one each; H.V. Burlingham (1010), W.S. Yeates (1011), Thomas Harrington (1012), Willowbrook (1014), whilst 1013 and 1015 went to Vauxhall's Export Department. However, there were a number of changes in the bodying industry at that time, notably Duple's takeover of both Burlingham (to form Duple Northern) and Willowbrook (to form Duple Midland). A plan to put an Alpine Continental body on 1010 at Duple Northern was abandoned on account of the expense, and chassis 1010 was sent to Loughborough instead.

Above: *Leon of Finningley were for decades one of the principle fare-stage operators to serve the routes outside Doncaster. Leon also operated tours and excursions, and chose the quite appropriate 448 VAL registration for this 1964 coach.*

This ostensibly meant that Duple now had three chassis to body as a service bus, and this was quite illogical. Plaxton's meanwhile, were complaining that they needed another chassis, "as a large tour operator wanted a model for evaluation prior to placing a considerable order." Vauxhall therefore reclaimed 1014, and Dave Sayer drove the bare chassis to Scarborough in an atrocious snowstorm in January 1963. Eventually, 1014 was bodied and used as a demonstrator on Vauxhall registration plates, before being supplied with two production chassis to Wallace Arnold. Willowbrook were later compensated, when they were given permission to create an 'official' Bedford B53F bus demonstrator on either production chassis 1246 or 1247.

Duple got the lion's share of the VAL allocations because of their long association with Chevrolet and Bedford. Indeed, their Hendon premises were just down the road from the General Motors' Chevrolet plant, and even when production was duly transferred to Luton this long association remained unbroken! Following the introduction of the new Bedford WHB chassis, Duple became the main body builder on the Marque during the 1930s, as the succeeding WLB and WTB models went through Hendon in large numbers, followed by the early OB model, despite the end of normal OB production at the outbreak of war.

From 1942 onwards, the Ministry of Supply (MoS) allowed Bedford to recommence the manufacturer of a single-deck OWB bus. Duple (and its licensees) was the only builder that was allowed by the MoS to construct single-deck bodies. The OB was re-introduced with 29-seat Duple Vista bodywork in 1945 and thousands were made before production ended in 1951. This set into position the Bedford-Duple combination that many post-war coach companies built their business upon.

When Bedford launched the 33-seat SB chassis in 1950, Duple designed the new Vega body, the first type to be fitted on an SB. A succession of Vega bodies appeared on the SB models that followed during the 1950s. For the 1960s, Duple introduced a harmonious range of new styles. Principally designed for fitting to the Bedford VAS, VAL14 and the later VAM, these bodies were respectively Bella Vista, Vega Major and the Bella Vega. Duple was chosen to construct the coachwork on the first prototype VAL14 chassis Bedford released. This was RHD62/2 (registered 825 CYR) and fitted with the Vega Major style of bodywork with seating for 52 passengers. This remained as a Bedford-Duple demonstrator until April 1963, when its role was supplanted by chassis 1201, which was fitted with a revised 52-seat Vega Major body (HMJ 828).

Top Right: *Overland of Preston took chassis number 1032 into stock during March 1963, with Vega Major body 1158/14. It carries the earlier style body with the rear-end 'flash'.*

Middle Right: *A styling change to the Vega Major eliminated the short flash on the rear flanks, as seen on ADC 195B, which was new to Begg's of Thornaby in March 1964.*

Bottom Right: *Internal changes were made for 1965, as shown by DJU 706C, one of a pair new to Gibson's of Barlestone. It will be noted from this selection of photographs that the Duple Vega Major could be ordered with or without cant-rail roof lights.*

Above: *This view shows the Embassy-bodied VAL (7999 MD) that Plaxton exhibited at the 1962 Commercial Motor Show. With its multiple window bays and forced-air ventilation, it was new to Bloomfields (part of the World Wide Coach group), and is seen on an Omnibus Society tour in 1963.* John Bristow

Catering for the burgeoning coach travel market of the 1960s was not the sole prerogative of Duple, and their main rivals were Plaxton's, based at Scarborough on the North Yorkshire coast. Fred Plaxton's business has, at the time of writing, just celebrated their centenary but back in the 1950s, their main offering had been the Consort and Venturer body ranges.

A number of these had been fitted on the Bedford SB models, but it wasn't until the end of the latter part of the 1950s that the Bedford Bus & Truck Plant, by then having moved from Luton to Dunstable, had sufficient capacity to produce chassis in any volume for the other coach builders. Quite simply, during the 1940s and 1950s, Hendon had soaked up the majority of the PSV chassis produced at Luton for the home market, as well as dealing with quite a few export ones as well.

It is reported that there was also something of an underlying problem between Plaxton and Bedford, as the Yorkshire firm had exhibited a marked reluctance to carry the Bedford badge on the front of their bodies. Former senior Bedford managers recall that whilst this problem was not as prominent during the 1950s as it became some years later, they nevertheless felt that this was a constant source of tension that was ready to erupt at almost any time.

Always distinctive, and in some ways unique, the Plaxton range was ready for a sea-change by the late-1950s, and the impetus for change came when Sheffield United Tours approached the firm for a new style of touring coach. The SUT Manager, Ben Goodfellow, wanted to have six AEC Reliance chassis bodied with a better view of the passing landscape than would normally be afforded by a conventional coach body of the period. The result was a body that utilised the standard front and rear of existing models, but had three window panels that were not only deeper than those on the Consort but roughly double the length as well. An example, known as the Panorama Pioneer appeared in the 1958 British Coach Rally.

The Panorama was developed for the 1958 Commercial Motor Show with a two-piece windscreen and side windows that then measured 6' 8" x 2' 8". Development continued during the 1959 and 1960 seasons, and experimental chassis RHD62/3 was fitted with a variant of the Panorama body, which was known as the Plaxton VAL. However, problems with excess vibration on the window panels and water leaks in the roof caused Plaxton to re-think their strategy and the body was stripped off the chassis and it was sent to Luton, where it was found that there was a distortion in one of the chassis members.

Meanwhile, the 1960 Commercial Motor Show saw Plaxton launch their Embassy range and it was decided that a version of this body would be used on chassis 1009 for Bloomfields Coaches Ltd., of Camberwell Road, London. Registered 7999 MD, it was shown at the 1962 Commercial Motor Show, illustrating a mixture of the Embassy and Panorama styles.

Although the makers had opted for the Embassy design, the majority of customers at the stand expressed an interest in the Panorama body. As a result, Plaxton rapidly modified the design of the Plaxton VAL and fitted a 'new' Panorama body on chassis 1004. This appeared as a near-side drawing in *The Commercial Motor* of 2nd November 1962, showing the side windows with three large panels and two smaller ones at the rear.

The VAL body was not scrapped, but languished at Eastgate for a while, before it was united with RHD62/1 which had been shipped up from MCW, due to the poor sales performance of the Topaz. Vauxhall were wanting to promote their cars by motor racing competitions and it was decided that the chassis could be used as a transporter. As the Plaxton VAL body survived at Scarborough, this was to be modified to suit the purpose.

Top Right: *Photographed during its youth and looking superb in the livery of its first owner, Finglands of Rusholme, 518 XJ, stands patiently awaiting it's patrons. The coach was a 1964 example of the VAL14 and was built with the early Plaxton Panorama style of bodywork with seating for 49-passengers.*

Middle Right: *Where but Blackpool could make a 36' (11m) long coach look small? Tatlock of Whitefield's VAL14 (DTC 563B) Edith III was built on chassis 1346 and supplied new with Panorama bodywork in 1964. Vauxhall Motors*

Bottom Right: *The early bodies had double sliding vents in the first and third bays, but many users began to demand air-conditioning; including Scott's Greys who bought one of the 'forced air' Panorama models (166 XHN) in 1964.*

Above: *Thomas Harrington of Hove came up with their Legionnaire design for the VAL, and it is believed that this is their first offering on chassis demonstrator 1012, but no subsequent PSV owner is recorded. Note the Legionnaire script on the rear side panels! This body was later fitted to a production chassis after the demonstrator chassis was recalled.* Vauxhall Motors

After the Duple take-over of Burlingham and Willowbrook, the only other contenders for bodying chassis were Harringtons, Metro-Cammell-Weymann and Yeates. Harrington had been building luxury coaches for decades, their products were particularly in vogue with many operators in the south of England, including Southdown and many of the London coach operators. The introduction of Harrington's superb Cavalier and the vaguely similar Grenadier coach bodies, (intended to clothe the underfloor engine chassis such as the AEC Reliance and Leyland Leopard) greatly enhanced the firm's reputation. Then, with the introduction of the VAL chassis, Harrington designed their new Legionnaire style of coachwork, and were supplied with chassis 1012 as a demonstrator model by Bedford.

These demonstrators were all owned by Vauxhall Motors, but they were used by the coachbuilders to gain orders after the 1962 Commercial Motor Show; many of them were eventually sold to operators in the spring of 1963. After the body was removed from 1012, the chassis went back to Dunstable and this may be the unit sent to GM in Canada minus its engine.

The Legionnaire had a distinctive body with a large radiator grille, slender window pillars and restrained trim. In all, it was a marked contrast to the more rakish styling of the Cavalier and Grenadier models. The Legionnaire did utilise the Grenadier's fibreglass rear panel, but in order to allow the maximum height for the windows, they sacrificed the glass panel that normally displayed the operator's name. Accordingly, this was placed in a separate 'light box' and fitted on the 'shelf' behind the rear seat so that it could be seen through the rear screen. The boot was huge, so much so, that two access hatches were provided on each side to supplement the 'patent' Harrington cantilever boot lid. As with previous models, the aluminium trim used around the outside waist-rail was supplied by the German firm Happische. However, for the Legionnaire, Harrington used a wider design of trim that had not been seen in the UK before.

For the 1965 model year, the MkII Legionnaire was shown at the 1964 Commercial Motor show. The main difference was the change to the curve of the roof, which adopted the shallow curve used on the Grenadier. Consequently, the interior headroom and luggage space was reduced! Like the Grenadier, the MkII could be ordered with four perspex glazed panels set in the roof, but this led to the interior becoming infamously hot!

Among the customers who chose the Legionnaire were Barton who took eight as their fleet numbers 989-996 (989-96 VRR). Meanwhile, Yelloway of Rochdale also purchased four in 1965 (CDK 409-12C). In regard to this firm, it is rather unusual, as they took in Plaxton Panorama-bodied VALs at the same time. Quite why they chose two suppliers is not known.

Several minor tour operators, such as Heaps Tours of Leeds also chose the Legionnaire over the more popular designs that were offered by Duple and Plaxton. Heaps' examples were a pair with 'Leopard skin' moquette registered CNW 154-5C; the reason for this, was due to the fact that Heaps had a leaping Leopard as their company motif. Harrington only made 58 Legionnaire bodies (all kinds of chassis before they ceased business at the end of 1965.

Willowbrook were not a big producer either, and after chassis 1014 went to Plaxton it was fitted with a Panorama body loaned to Wallace Arnold, before it was sold to them in May 1963 as 132 FUA, along with a pair of later chassis (1136 and 1138 - 133-4 FUA). Willowbrook then bodied 1199 (4940 ET) in October 1963, before receiving chassis 1246-7 as possible demonstrators. Of these, 1246, was taken over by Vauxhall and registered 525 LMJ, but 1247 (3170 NT) was not adopted and thus sold to an operator. Commencing with 1276 (351 CYG) early in 1964, isolated examples followed in the years ahead, five on VAL14s and 11 VAL70s: Wigmore of Dinnington were the biggest devotee of the Willowbrook VAL.

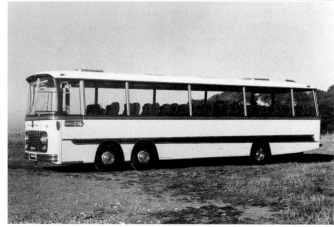

Top Right: *Emphasising the styling at the back of the MkI body, and its severe roof line, is DEV 66B. This was one of a pair new to Harris Coaches of Grays (DEV 65-6B), and it is seen at the 1964 Brighton Coach Rally.*

Middle Right: *A Legionnaire patiently awaits restoration, but disregarding the missing radiator grille cover, compare the coach at the top of this page.* Tony J. Griffin

Bottom Right: *Although a similar looking view to that on the top of page 12, this is in fact the MkII Legionnaire of 1965, as noted by the more curved roof line.* Vauxhall Motors

The next firm to consider as furnishers of the VAL14 chassis, were the Loughborough coach building firm founded by William Stanley Yeates. This company was responsible for creating some of the most flamboyant British coach designs, especially with their Riviera, Europa and Fiesta designs. Their radical and distinctive styling was particularly evident during the 1950s, although prior to that period, the coaches turned out were much more in keeping with their competitors save for the rather florid side flash. A Fiesta body was applied to demonstrator chassis 1011. During the 1960s, Yeates bodied several VAL chassis on the Europa and Fiesta designs, but of these only the dual-door coach (966 RVO), which was part of a seven-strong batch new to Barton of Chilwell in 1963, is known to have lasted into preservation.

Below: *This Yeates-bodied VAL 14 was new to the fleet of Gibson Brothers, Barlestone, who traded as Comfort. Using the Fiesta body, 407 EAY features a sloping window pillar style that differentiates it from the Europa model.*

The well-known firm of Metro-Cammell-Weymann also produced a body for the VAL14, known as the Topaz, which was rather a continental-inspired affair with a peaked roof over the windscreen. There was only one such example of the design, which was used as a demonstrator on prototype Bedford VAL chassis RHD 62/1. But, as the picture on the opposite page shows, it was nowhere near as stylish as the offerings from Weymann's competitors.

As a consequence, the rather bland-looking coach attracted only a limited interest and no real sales. Vauxhall, concerned at the lack of progress in orders being obtained by Weymann, came up with an edict to 'get moving or send the chassis back!' In the end, Dave Sayer recalls being sent to collect the chassis from Addlestone, and got a stormy reception on his arrival.

As mentioned earlier, it was originally the intention of Vauxhall to use this with their own in-house racing team, but for one reason after another it never progressed any further, although in 1964 an Australian racing driver called Denis (Denny) Hulme approached Vauxhall about the vehicle's future.

The original body languished at the MCW works for a while, but it was eventually put on chassis 1183, and sold to Rowson of Hayes in July 1963 as BMK 354A. Later MCW introduced their 'Topaz II' design, which were all delivered from the Addlestone factory in 1965. The first body was placed on chassis 1280 as a demonstrator (but this was not Vauxhall approved) and eventually sold to Clarke of London (as KRO 545C) that October at a reduced price. The other chassis were bodied in May, June and July as follows: 1416 (Davies, Tredeger; FAX 8C), 1420 (Jones, Aberbeeg; FAX 314C), 1439 (Wallace Arnold; CUM 494C), 1441 (Billies of Mexborough; FWW 809C), and lastly 1471 (Fox, Hayes; JNK 686C).

Above: *Seen at the 1962 Commercial Motor Show, is chassis RHD62/1, with the unique Topaz body. It was registered 472 DYK and used as a demonstrator for a short while.* MCW

Right: *Whilst the Topaz II, was a totally different design, it fared little better. Photographed at Pond Street, Sheffield in the 1970s was this example of the MCW Topaz II, which went to Billies of Mexborough as FWW 809C.* Tony J. Griffin

CENTRE STAGE

Whilst the Chevrolet and early Bedford bus chassis had carried luxury bodies, during the 1920s and 1930s it was more common for the vehicles to be purchased primarily as service buses. During this period, at a time when rail travel still accounted for most holiday and excursion traffic, the majority of the Bedfords sold went for rural bus work. This often did include a percentage of touring and excursion work, but it wasn't until after World War II that this began to change.

By the 1950s, the slogan that Bedford had applied to its truck range from the 1930s onwards, "You see them everywhere", quite appropriately was applied to the bus range. Many operators had examples of the OB or OWB in their fleets, and some even went on to convert their wartime buses to serve as dual-purpose service buses and touring coaches, using them on fare stage during the week and evening or weekend tours.

Above: *Leon of Finningley operated various bus services in the Doncaster area, and for these routes they purchased (in 1964) ARR 720B, a VAL14 with Duple Midland bus bodywork.*

Principally the chassis of the normal stage service single-deck bus is identical to that used on a contemporary coach, the overall difference was really in the type of bodywork and interior that was fitted, which was stipulated by the customer. Many rural bus and coach firms grew up on the Bedford brand, and it therefore came as no surprise when the VAL14 chassis started appearing in the role of the conventional service bus. It is only questionable as to why Bedford were reluctant to authorise an official conversion, especially as chassis 1008, 14 were initially allocated for a service bus bodying. For this role, and fitted with a cheaper body style, they were a superbly economical piece of equipment; having a large seating capacity and relatively low running costs.

At 52- to 54-seat capacity, the VAL14 service bus was almost comparable with traditional double-deck buses and many of the firms that purchased them benefited further by using one-man-operation. The combination of the 6.17-litre Leyland engine and a frugal body, meant purchase cost-savings of almost £1,500 per service bus. The combination also gave a better fuel consumption at around 15-17mpg. The VAL14 service bus solved some thorny problems for many rural operators, most frequently on routes where damage was caused to double-deck roofs by overhanging tree branches. But none of these difficulties were as profound as that on the North Western Road Car's No.98 route! At Dunham Woodhouse the route passed under a very low bridge on the Bridgewater Canal, and even normal single-deck service buses had problems. Rather than try to send a square peg through a round hole, they looked at the low-chassis height VAL to see if it could resolve their problem.

This resulted in Strachan's bodybuilders designing and constructing ten special-bodied 52-seat front-entrance buses. The first pair of these were delivered in July 1964 and the other eight followed in August. The roofs on these buses were particularly rounded and curved from the centre line to virtually the top of the side windows. These ten buses were then registered AJA 130-139B, with corresponding fleet numbers, and were painted in the traditional red and cream fleet livery of the company. The smart bodywork utilised a double curvature windscreen, below which was a rather large radiator grille with stacked headlights close by on either side.

Although the North West Road Car order for Strachan bodies remained unique, other firms like Marshall and Willowbrook all produced service bus bodies. In 1968 Plaxton are reputed to have offered an experimental version of their Derwent body for OK Motor Services, yet this was never fitted to the allocated VAL70 chassis, although nobody seems to know why this was.

Top Right: *The most common service bus bodies on the VAL14 chassis were those by Duple (Midland). This vehicle was supplied new to Richmond of Epsom and registered 4230 PE. Some years later, it was photographed whilst serving in South Yorkshire with the Fords of Ackworth fleet.*

Middle Right: *In service 1964 is North Western Road Car Co. 136 (AJA 136B) is working the 41 Hale Barns route, showing the Strachan-bodied VALs had a wide use.* John G. Kaye

Bottom Right: *Burton of Brixham's VAL14 (COD 925C) was built with a Marshall body in 1965.*

Walter Lord, states that, "Plaxton Director Fred Ford, who had also been involved with the trans-Atlantic 'Flxible' project, had wanted to extend the service bus bodying activities of the company, and this had seen the re-introduction of the Derwent name in 1966, although it had briefly featured in Plaxton's range in 1962." This is not the place to go into the internal politics of the Scarborough firm, but it is significant that Ford left the firm in the Spring of 1968 and the Flxible project was rapidly dropped, and therefore the VAL/Derwent concept may have been another casualty. The VAL70 chassis was returned to Bedford, along with covering correspondence, from which it could be seen that OK Motors (a long-standing Plaxton customer) were exceptionally disappointed by the whole affair.

Top Left: *Willowbrook was another company that had managed for decades to acquire a reputation for quality bus and coach bodies, although it was eventually taken over by Duple in 1960. The early Duple and Willowbrook styles then became very similar for a time, but the use of a large oblong radiator and a plain front did little to enhance the looks of these bodies. This bus in this photograph, (525 LMJ) was built on VAL14 chassis number 1246 by Willowbrook in 1963 and was for a while used as a demonstrator by Vauxhall Motors.*

Middle Left: *Willowbrook were later sold off by Duple, and in 1969 they produced this dual-purpose body on a VAL70 chassis number 7T460118. By this time an improved trim and more attractive front end was evident on the service bus delivered to Tailby & George of Willington in October 1968. A second 56-seat dual-purpose vehicle was acquired five months later, and this was registered BRB 674G. This company was far better known as Blue Bus of Willington, and was held in great esteem by staff and customers alike. Sadly the firm suffered a disastrous depot fire on 5th January 1976 and this brought about its eventual demise.*

Bottom Left: *The Ulster Transport Authority (UTA) was another example of an operator with a small demand for a large-capacity vehicle. One Bedford VAL chassis was exported across the Irish Sea in 1964, where it was bodied by the UTA themselves as a 56-seat bus. This was a rather bland affair from a stylist's point of view, but then again its role was based on the merits of a functional vehicle rather than that of a luxury touring coach. The bus was registered as 2318 GZ, and given the fleet number 118. It is seen here in Bangor on 22nd September 1969. John Bristow*

MEMORIES OF THE VAL AT WORK

When this book was in its early stages I found myself perusing the photographs of a hot summer holiday spent on the Isle of Wight nearly 30-years ago. This was a coach tour holiday operated by Robinsons of Great Harwood, who themselves had operated VAL models, including Vega Major-bodied CTD 323-5B in their green and black livery.

I knew that the island was then a haven for the Bedford VAL, with various models still being used on local tours even at what was then a late date in their lives. Among them was PDL 823H; this was one of the later Duple-bodied examples and had been new to Seaview Services. It was in the Regent Coaches livery at that time but the vehicle was still in a really splendid condition. Southern Vectis being the main operator on the island understandably had taken several early examples of the VAL models for use on their 'round the island tours'. They expanded their fleet of VAL coaches further in 1966 when Duple-bodied 403-5 (EDL 992-4D) were taken into stock. Then a further four (HDL 228-31E) followed in 1967.

Above: *In the late-1970s, the Isle of Wight was still a mecca for enthusiasts who wanted to closely observe the Bedford VAL in everyday use. Among the fleet of the principle tour operator, Southern Vectis, were examples of these Duple bodied VALs like HDL 228E. The other vehicle, OOR 320G was a VAL70 from the grey and red-liveried West Wight of Totlands Bay. This coach had been acquired in 1971 from Gale of Halesmere.*

Most of the other tour operators that were based on the island competed with the nationalised undertaking by introducing the model to their fleets; as for example Moss Motor Tours of Sandown (ADL 252B), whose coaches were finished in a dual blue and white livery. This company later acquired EDL 783D, which had originally been a Vauxhall Motors Demonstrator and had been exhibited at the 1964 World's Fair in New York.

Perhaps one of the more unusual examples of the VAL seen at a holiday resort was ADL 321B, as this was one of the Duple Midland service bus examples. This vehicle was rather colourful for a bus, painted as it was in the traditional Seaview Services livery of two shades of green and red.

Top Left: *Photographed while on a private hire duty is one of the 1964 examples of the Southern Vectis Bedford VAL14 coaches. This batch were all fitted with the very popular Duple Vega Major coachwork. While still in the first flush of youth and wearing its original livery, ADL 110B basks quietly in the Isle of Wight sunshine. Note the unusual side panel name plate, which was not very common on this bodywork.*

Middle Left: *Southern Vectis (ADL 109B), Bedford VAL14 is seen here at Ryde in the company of other tour operators. The Bedford marque was very popular on the Isle of Wight, with many different models being operated there. The coach behind this VAL is one of the many Duple Super Vega-bodied Bedford SB models that could be found on the island into the 1980s.*

Bottom Left: *The traditional colour scheme of Southern Vectis was a rather smart green and cream livery, but in common with most of the state-owned bus and coach businesses, they lost their individual identity in the 1970s. During that era, the bus liveries changed to 'Poppy Red' or 'Leaf Green'. Coaches like ADL 109B on the other hand, even if still proclaiming an identity like Black & White or Royal Blue, were painted in an overall white livery with 'National' fleet names consisting of alternate red and blue lettering.*

The VAL service bus had been purchased in 1964 as a replacement for a Leyland Titan PD2, the last of a pair that was in the Seaview fleet at that time as Seaview Services were the last of the independent operators on the island to operate a stage service. This service was operated to the holiday resort of Ryde. Prior to using these Titans on stage carriage duties, Seaview had operated other double deck-buses, among them one that had, come from as far away as the Rochdale Corporation fleet.

The VAL however was very much a worthwhile choice, as the seating accommodation was very similar to the retired double-deck bus; the Titan having had a low-bridge 53-seat Leyland body, whilst the VAL was a 54-seat saloon. Seaview catered for their tourist business too, as two months later they took into stock BDL 214B, which was a Plaxton-bodied coach version of the VAL14.

Then, as if to pick up the gauntlet thrown down by Southern Vectis, who had just acquired its next batch of VALs. Seaview acquired another VAL14 (HDL 454E). Among other island operators, the VAL found favour with Shotters of Brighstone (who took both a Duple and a Plaxton bodied example in 1967) and the aforementioned Moss Motor Tours of Sandown.

20

During the mid-1960s, when I began to start paying more detailed attention to buses and coaches, my father was working as a bodybuilder for Hanson Buses Ltd. of Huddersfield, having served his apprenticeship as a coachbuilder with Charles H. Roe of Crossgates, Leeds. As a result I became well aware of the VAL chassis, even though Hanson employed mostly AEC, Ford or Bedford SB chassis. Quite why they never adopted the VAL surprised me, especially when local rival Baddeley Brothers of Holmfirth purchased first a trio of Vega Major-bodied examples (65 EWT in 1963 and BWY 709-10B in 1964) then a pair of Plaxton Panoramas (FYG 918-920C) in 1965.

The arrival of these five VAL14s saw Baddeley's undertaking some interesting long-distance excursion tours, with destinations like Edinburgh, Great Yarmouth and Weston-Super-Mare. The VALs just loved motorway work, and even in the event of a front tyre blow-out, the coach could be brought to a controlled stop and, if required, even be driven normally for a short distance to a motorway service area. Such an event happened to Alan Earnshaw (my Editor) in 1970 when he was working as a driver's assistant on a Baddeley VAL70 (YWU 292G) just south of Forton Services on the M6 whilst heading for the Lake District. Baddeley's had four VAL70s, the last arriving in 1971 as JWT 725J. One of the earlier VAL14s (BWY 710B) gave stirling service, lasting in the fleet until just after the West Yorkshire PTE took over the firm in 1976. Another Huddersfield example worked with Ward Brothers of Lepton.

Top Right: *Baddeley Brothers of Holmfirth No.73 (65 EWT), lasted in service with the firm for seven years, when it was replaced by VAL70 No.106 (DWR 461H).*
John Locke collection

Middle Right: *Although buyers in the PSV market had a lot less say in the external appearances of their new coach after World War II, this was certainly not true of the lavish internal appointments. This photograph shows just one of the variations in the internal appearance of the Duple Vega Major luxury coachwork as fitted to the VAL chassis. Looking to the rear of the coach the picture shows how inviting the interior was and with the coach being provided with netting luggage racks, the cant-rail window lights are far less impeded.* Duple

Bottom Right: *This is an interesting image, in that it shows a highly confidential experiment undertaken by Duple at Hendon, whereby they fitted Plaxton-style trim and seating for 48 passengers to a Vega Major body.* Duple

Top Left: *Seen outside the Ramsden Street offices of the* Huddersfield Examiner *in April 1963 is 773 DWW. The VAL14, just having been delivered from the Plaxton factory for Ward Brothers - Red Lion Coaches, Lepton. It was one of a batch of five ordered via the dealers, Hughes of Cleckheaton. The others were 772 DWW (Mosley Barugh Green), 65 EWT (Baddeley Brothers), 134 EWW (Gray, Hoyland Common) and 486 DWY (Guisley Tours, Yeadon).* Huddersfield Examiner

Centre Left: *Local to my area, Wallace Arnold of Leeds had a pick-up point on Huddersfield's Venn Street, and I recall the 49-seat Plaxton-bodied coaches calling there quite regularly. This one, 232 HUM had Plaxton body 642182 on chassis 1351. It lasted in the fleet until April 1971.*

Bottom Left: *Another regular visitor to Huddersfield was West Riding's trio of Plaxton-bodied VAL14s (2980 HL and 2997-8HL. We see here fleet number 998 (2998 HL).* John L Kaye

Huddersfield, was just one area that I saw first hand, but the VAL also saw service worldwide. However, we have not concerned ourselves with export models of the VAL in this publication, as there is simply not enough space or available information for us to do so. With production numbers reaching over 2,000 PSV examples, the vehicle had its greatest impact here in the United Kingdom. However, we might mention some of the destinations that the model was exported to. Subsequent to the earlier *Bedford Buses* books, readers have told us that these overseas destinations included Australia, Belgium, Denmark, Eire, Egypt, Finland, Fiji, Holland, India, Iran, Iraq, New Zealand, Northern Ireland, Norway, Pakistan, Russia, Saudi Arabia, South Africa, Sweden and Turkey.

Bedford also had hopes that the VAL might sell well in Europe, and one of the demonstrator chassis 1013, which had been intended for bodying as a service bus, was sent to Finland and bodied by Kuopion in 1964, meanwhile, intended as a dual-purpose bus chassis 1015 was sent to General Motors in Denmark, but there is no record of what it became after it reached Copenhagen in 1962. It is said another VAL chassis (number not known but possibly 1012), was sent to General Motors in Canada. Nearer home, quite a number of VALs were shipped to the Isle of Man, and it is believed that between 16 and 18, both VAL14 and VAL70 models were shipped as second-hand vehicles to the attractive island in the Irish Sea; three of these then went on for further lives in Northern Ireland.

There are strongly conflicting figures on the number of VAL chassis put on the road, as not all were registered as PSVs, and the export figures also appear to be contradictory. It is generally agreed that just over 2,000 Bedford VAL chassis were bodied for the British PSV industry, and that the vast majority of these were fitted with various succeeding examples of coachwork from either the Duple or the Plaxton design studios.

By the end of their production lives in early 1973 the VAL, like its Bedford predecessors, could "be seen everywhere"! Like the 1964 example in the Baddeley Brothers fleet (BWY 710B), that my Editor almost bought in 1976 (but was outbid on at the last minute), some operators got well over ten-years service out of their purchases. This was quite remarkable for a 'cheap chassis', especially given some of the problems that the early models were plagued with (such as the braking system), but which have been deliberately 'glossed over' in this rose-tinted tribute.

Their longevity in service could be traced to the relative cheapness of many components, for the VAL employed many of the items used in the Bedford truck ranges, especially the TK model. As such, these were both mass produced and widely available. Second, third, fourth and even fifth users of VALs were quite common, and both VAL14s and VAL70s stayed in service with coach operators well into the 1980s. Even after their working PSV days were over, a large number of VAL chassis were to be seen converted into caravans, horse boxes and stock/racing car transporters due to their low-height floors.

Below: *This photograph illustrates that, although the Vega Major design, went through a styling change during the mid-1960s, the later models still inherited the diagonal rear pillar that was a styling feature. This 1966 VAL14 (JAC 25D), whilst photographed in the livery of Upwell & District Coaches, was originally owned by Smith of Long Itchington.*

Above: *The firm of Thomas Harrington & Co. of Hove produced the above Legionnaire design for the VAL chassis. Not many were built, but the well-known Yelloway fleet of Rochdale had the MkII Legionnaire-bodied coaches registered CKD 408-12C. Contrary to the common story, Harrington was never part of the Rootes Group, although the family did take a financial stake in the firm in 1961. This came about when the Robins & Day Group, which was owned by the Rootes family, purchased the Hove-based business.Conversions on the Commer minibus highlighted a Rootes connection with Harrington's Sackville Works in Hove until coachbuilding ceased there at the end of 1965. Thereafter, Plaxton took over the supply of replacement glass, along with the panel repairs for Harrington bodies, so most of Hove's fibreglass moulds went to Scarborough.* Yelloway Museum Archive

Before progressing further, it is incumbent upon me to mention that two VAL14s gained immortality in the movie world; with 1245, a Legionnaire-bodied (ALR 453B ex-Batten Coaches) starring in the *Italian Job* and the Plaxton-bodied URO 913E in the Beatles' *Magical Mystery Tour*. At the start of the Steve McQueen film *Le Mans*, the opening sequence of the movie shows the coach park with at least one VAL present.

Meanwhile, Norwich City Football Club used a Panorama-bodied VAL that was painted in green and yellow stripes to represent the club's kit and it even had green-tinted windows. Another famous Legionnaire CNW 155C, was purchased by Trans-Pennine for Vauxhall Heritage. Unfortunately, Vauxhall Heritage eventually decided that the Harrington project was too big to undertake in the time available, and a Duple-bodied Bedford was then restored; allowing the Harrington (seen on the cover) to be passed to Cyril Kenzie for restoration.

Duple Motor Bodies meanwhile had acquired the Yeates coachbuilding concern of Loughborough in 1963. Yeates then concentrated on the sales and marketing of buses and coaches for the second-hand market. Neither of these situations affected the marketing of the Bedford VAL, as Duple and Plaxton had long been the only choice for the majority of VAL customers.

Above: *In County Durham there were many independent bus companies that operated vehicles that could be used on private hire or excursion and also for stage services. One of these was Wade Emmerson's OK Motor Services of Bishop Auckland. Among the vehicles new to this fleet in 1965 was VAL14 (GUP 703C), which is a very interesting example as it shows one of the last Panorama variants to keep the sliding windows. These opening window models were retained for a short while until fixed window air-conditioned versions became standard.*

Right: *Contrasting with the above Plaxton coach with its very simple lines, the Duple Vega Major body somehow takes on a less perpendicular stance. Eagle Line of Swindon took this coach into stock in July 1963; the vehicle later passed to Brice of Four Marks in 1973.*

Above: *This Yeates Europa-bodied Bedford VAL 14, 964 RVO was one of a batch of coaches and dual-purpose buses supplied new to Barton of Chilwell in the summer of 1963. This view of fleet number 964 shows the livery without the large IN and OUT wording alongside the doors.* John L. Kaye

Left: *Heaps Tours of Leeds purchased two Harrington Legionnaire-bodied VAL14 coaches, the second of which (CNW 155C) has had an eventful life. After being withdrawn from the Heaps fleet this coach was taken into stock by John Wood of Wold Newton who operated the vehicle for some time until the front screen was damaged in a yard shunting exercise. As the glass was no longer available, it was stored in a shed for a number of years until it was 'discovered' by one of the Trans-Pennine team.* Alan Earnshaw

Above: *Starkly contrasting with the Yeates body opposite, Plaxton were one of the few coachbuilders that remained with the more curvaceous styling throughout the evolution of the Panorama model. This West Riding Road Car, VAL 14, (EHL 472D) was a superb 1966 example of the model. This vehicle was often seen working south of Wakefield on the M1, and my Editor recalls working with Baddeley's VAL14/Panorama FYG 920C which was on hire to WRCC. In consort with EHL 472D the pair did a tour of the Lincolnshire bulb fields in 1968.*

Right: *This 1966 VAL14 (EFA 494D) is displayed in the livery of its original owner, Viking of Burton-on-Trent. This example is built with the later style of Duple Vega Major body that was introduced for the 1966 season, although this particular coach only had seating for 49 passengers.*

Above: *The lavish and extravagant styling of the Caetano Estoril coachwork was one of the more unusual bodies that were fitted to the VAL chassis. This VAL 70 (STB 450G) was serving in the fleet of the continental tour operator Carnell Tours and dates from 1969. Note the illuminated side panel above the front wheels, the distinctive style of paintwork and the curtained windows.*

Left: *Whilst unregistered in this photograph, this new VAL70 was an early example of the new Plaxton Panorama Elite style of luxury coach work. Whilst being delivered on trade plates (395 DK) chassis number 7T459398 would become HNK 149G. Destined for the Sonners fleet at Chatham in March 1969, the coach was actually built on a late-1968 chassis.* Plaxton

THE LARGER FLEET USERS

As mentioned earlier, it was rather surprising when the North Western Road Car Company made the decision to purchase the Strachan bodied VAL14s for the special needs of their route through Dunham Woodhouse. It was unusual for such a company to consider the Bedford marque, for Bedford had seldom been a chassis that was to be found in either the fleets of the municipal concerns or indeed the larger well known stage operators. North Western Road Car, for example, was firmly entrenched in the Lancashire area and having its origins in the British Automobile Traction Company, the business had been quite happy with the various offerings from Leyland even though the fleet also contained models of AEC, Albion and Dennis manufacture during the 1960s.

Above: *During 1963 Wallace Arnold placed a small trial order with a Plaxton -bodied Bedford Demonstrator and two production line VAL14 coaches, with further orders being placed in succeeding years. Among the 1965 intake was BNW 617C, which was allocated to the firm's Feathers Tours fleet.*

One operator who had traditionally used more expensive underfloor engined coaches was Wallace Arnold, and whilst they had used Bedford chassis such as the OB and SB in the past, they began testing the large-capacity offering from Bedford by placing a rather tentative order for three VAL14 chassis with Plaxton Panorama bodies in 1963 (132-134 FUA), which included the re-bodied demonstrator chassis 1014 and two later models. These were all equipped with Plaxton 52-seat bodies, but experience on touring work showed these were too cramped.

Top Left: *During an excursion to Blackpool we see Yelloway's first pair of VALs (6693-4 DK), which were fitted with Plaxton bodywork. A book on Yelloway's is shortly to appear in the Fare Stage Series. Yelloway Museum Archives*

Middle Left: *Barton employed a large number of dual-purpose bodies, including three 56-seat dual door bodies by Yeates in 1963, along with four Yeates C50D Europa coaches from the same maker. Alan Earnshaw*

Bottom Left: *Wallace Arnold purchased a very odd example in 1969, RUA 713G on a 1967 chassis (7T4591448), which may have been a VAL70 demonstrator. Their last order for six more VAL70s, was strangely cut back to three. The other three went to Cleckheaton dealers, Hughes, who sold two of them on to Baddeley Brothers (YWU 292-3G) and the other to Mosley of Barugh Green near Barnsley (YWU 615G). After that Wallace Arnold were finished with the VAL. Dave Haddock*

These next vehicles acquired by Wallace Arnold in March 1964 again had Plaxton bodies, but this batch of 17 (221-237 HUM) had seats for only 49 passengers. Wallace Arnold's Directors and their customers must have been well pleased with their coaches, for March 1965 saw a further repeat order that resulted in 17 more VALs; BNW 615-41C were bodied by Plaxton as either 49- or 51-seaters. Duple provided a 52-seat body for BNW 643C, and a Weymann Topaz II gave 52-seats on CUM 494C. In 1966 it was back to Plaxton for 17 more 49-seaters (EUG 904-16, 919 ,921 and 926-27D), and one 52-seater (EUM 401D). In 1967, five 52-seat Panorama coaches were purchased in the batch JUA 318-22E. A final VAL14 (chassis 7816727) was acquired along with three VAL70s in the batch MNW 700-3F in early 1968. In 1969, six VAL70s chassis were ordered with 53-seat Plaxton bodies, but the order was inexplicably cut back to just three (SUB 666-8G).

Wallace Arnold's acquisitions make an interesting case study, as they show how an experienced and highly professional operator (that normally used high class chassis) could utilise cheaper vehicles if the economies were right. Whilst the majority of firms buying the VAL tended to be smaller operators who had ambitions to break into the big time, they did appeal to some of the large private coach operators as well. Shearings, Yelloway of Rochdale, Don Everall of Wolverhampton, Maynard of Manchester, Barton of Chilwell and Rickard of Brentwood. They all took decent numbers of the VAL14 and some returned to place new orders for the VAL70.

Few of what would later become the National Bus Company constituents took the VAL in large numbers, but they were not entirely absent from either of the two big groups. One that operated the Bedford VAL was the relatively small Cumberland Motor Services, which was based in Whitehaven. They took a 1966 example with the MkII Vega Major bodywork, and employed this quite successfully on both private hire and tour work. A year later they returned for another two with Duple 51-seat bodies (LAO 580-1E). The Wakefield-based West Riding Automobile Company also started buying examples of the VAL14, doing so as early as 1963 with YHL 992-4 and then took subsequent examples as well.

As we have already discussed, they were well suited for tour work and stage carriage work, as the Southern Vectis operation on the Isle of Wight clearly discovered to their benefit. Also down south, Wilts & Dorset bought four VAL70s with 51-seat Duple bodies (LMR 731-4F) in 1968, and then got four more (PEL 903-6G) a year later. Neighbours Hants & Dorset purchased three coaches (ORU 579-81G) and another pair in July 1971 (WEL 802-3J). Meanwhile the Wiltshire undertaking had bought three more in May 1970 (SLJ 757-7H) and a further pair (WEL 804-5J) at the same time as Hants & Dorset's 1971 models. The Hants & Dorset coaching arm, Shamrock & Rambler had a Legionnaire (100 BRU) and subsequently took four Duple-bodied VAL70s in 1969 (PEL 994-7G).

Top Right: *This coach (100 BRU), was built on chassis 1325 and fitted with a Harrington Legionnaire body, to the original design and supplied new to Shamrock & Rambler of Bournemouth in March 1964. This company was primarily a fleet name used by Hants & Dorset.* Vauxhall Motors

Middle Right: *This view takes us back to the extreme south of the country and beyond the Solent to the Isle of Wight. Southern Vectis purchased their first pair of Duple Vega Major-bodied VAL 14s in 1964 for the tourist industry. These coaches (ADL 109-110B), were built on consecutive chassis 1493 and 1494.*

Bottom Right: *Cumberland Motor Services took this 1966 example of a Duple VAL14 into stock as fleet number 301. Like all coaches in that fleet, it was finished in the reversed livery of cream and red, the stage service fleet being in red with a cream trim. Alternatively other vehicles like the Bristol MW that is stood alongside GAO 38D were finished in the dual-purpose livery.*

Top Left: *Edinburgh Corporation were among the very few municipal operators with a sizeable fleet of coaches, which they employed on their city tours instead of conventional buses. Edinburgh were thus one of the few municipal bus fleets to chose the VAL14. Their first intake of the VAL were coaches 213-8 (213-8 SC) during January 1964.* Chris Taylor

Middle Left: *An unusual operator of the VAL14, Rhondda Transport was also one of the few municipal undertakings to invest in the twin-steer Bedford. This view of 395 WTG shows the Vega Major-bodied coach without chrome hub caps, a common indicator of over-heating brake drums.* Chris Taylor

Bottom Left: *One of Manchester's batch of D or E registered airport coaches (as yet un-registered) is seen prior to delivery in the blue and white livery outside the Plaxton works in Scarborough.* Manchester Museum of Transport

The municipal fleet operators were not big buyers of the VAL but the first to place an order was Rhondda Transport (1357-9). They ran these Duple-bodied coaches (395-7 WTG) for no less ten-years. One of them was even used to pick up a group called Tommy Scott and the Senators, who had been booked to play for the Transport Department's social club. Although you may not know the name, this singer (under a new stage name) bounced into the pop charts in 1965 with *Its Not Unusual*!

Edinburgh City Transport had a succession of VALs, starting in 1964 with 213-8 SC, which would last in the fleet until the 1970s, but they were supplemented by three VAL70s (MSF 223-5F), followed by another trio (PSC 228-30G) and fourth batch (SSF 235-7H) in May 1970. In August 1973, my Editor took a group to Heriott Watt University for a week. During the 'slack' time, two of the Baddeley Brothers' Ford R226 Duple Dominant coaches VWY 841/3L were loaned to Edinburgh (to try the Dominant body) and along with PSC 229G, the three ran daily tourist trips to Loch Katrine and the Trossachs.

In the north west of England, after a trial with a demonstrator, Manchester City Transport purchased three VAL14s in 1966 (GNB 516-8D), with three more (GND 111-113E) in 1967. Six of the early VAL 70s then arrived in April 1968, registered JND 207-12F. These, like the earlier models, were all supplied with Plaxton Panorama 1 bodies. The coaches were employed prominently on the Airport services like the final pair that were delivered later, (MND 213/4G). The services operated out of the then new Piccaddily Plaza, where the airport check-in desks and many airline offices were located near to the bus station.

NEW BODIES FOR OLD

As mentioned earlier, the two primary suppliers of coach bodies were Duple and Plaxton. Whilst Duple's 1962 offering was brand new, the Plaxton Panorama could be traced back to the late-1950s, and it was therefore not surprising when the company decided to refresh its image for the 1965 season.

In 1963 the company approached the innovative David Ogle Design Studios to take the design forward, but the main changes were to styling, rather than a complete re-vamp of the complete body. The first noticeable change being to the front end, wherein the former elongated oval chrome radiator cover was replaced by a very neat oblong pressing. Drivers particularly loved this styling change, as the mesh pressing used on the earlier VAL models had been a devil to clean and chrome polish.

Above: *The coach in the centre (GEF 595F) of this view, new to Beeline of Hartlepool, was an early example of the Duple Viceroy body. The early Plaxton Panorama bodied VAL on the left of this Bedford trio appears to be one of the six that were new to the Don Everall fleet of Wolverhampton in 1964. Whilst that on the SB chassis to the right is an example of a vehicle with the later Plaxton radiator style introduced in 1965.*

Pictures of the early style side of panels with the re-vamped front end, but still retaining the opening windows, are not all that common, but on page 25 we see an example of this change on a VAL14-Panorama supplied to OK Motor Services in 1965. The wider changes to the side panels soon followed with a ribbed chrome band that wrapped round the front and extended along the sides and as far back as the end of the first window bay.

Top Left: *In addition to Beeline of Hartlepool buying the Duple-bodied VAL14s (as seen on the previous page), the firm also acquired a second batch fitted with Plaxton Panorama coachwork. This illustration shows an overview of GEF 597F, with the new roof styling and the front end chrome trim clearly evident. Note will be taken of their very pleasant pale green and primrose livery, which was split in the roof at the third bay and was thus a deliberate styling feature at that time.* Vauxhall Motors

Middle Left: *A broad ribbed chrome band also featured below the one-piece rear window, as can be seen on the preserved King Alfred VAL14 (CCG 704C). It will also be observed that the small 'finned' rear wings on the earlier Panorama bodies have been replaced by four moulded housings to carry the circular rear light assemblies.*

Bottom Left: *I always thought that although they were still undoubtedly smart, by 1967, the coaches that came out of Plaxton were perhaps beginning to look a little dated. Tatlock's JTB 400F* (Edith) *seen at the Blackpool Coach Rally, when compared to the Duple coaches shown opposite, did not appear to be as modern; but that is of course a matter of personal opinion.* Vauxhall Motors

The 1966 Commercial Motor Show saw a change in the nonclementure of the Panorama models, with the forced-air versions and one-piece windows becoming known as the Panorama I, whilst those with the conventional sliding vents became the Panorama II. This was quite confusing, as it meant that there were in fact four successive Panorama I models.

A Panorama with shorter bays was also introduced in 1965 for fitting on the 32'-long Bedford VAM chassis. A number of these Panorama bodies did not have the broad chrome bands, and in some fleets there was a confusing mix of both types; Barton being a specific example, as vehicles in the LVO ***E series had chrome banded bodies on the AEC Reliance chassis and plain styling on the VAM5s. Further styling changes would come in 1967 when an experimental Panorama body was placed on road test, and this would appear as the Panorama Elite at the 1968 Commercial Motor Show. The Plaxton design team under Jack Mathers brought out a superb design, with curved side-windows, a practice that had been seen in private cars from the early 1960s. This therefore sorted out the confusion between the Panorama models, although the Panorama II remained in production for the SB range for some time after.

Duple on the other hand were not idle either, and after less than expected sales at the 1964 Commercial Motor Show, they began to look at improvements to their Vega/Vista range. It is perhaps a shame that they did not respond earlier, as the 1965 Panorama changes took quite a few customers northward to Yorkshire. Duple therefore took a view that a re-vamp to the existing range would act as a *pro-tem* stop-gap, but at the same time they were already designing two new coach bodies.

This bold step saw what would eventually become the Viceroy range being designed first, but as Alex Shaw remembers, the firm were already planning a completely new coach for the 1970s. This was to coincide with a decision to close the Hendon factory (announced in 1968), when all Duple coach production was concentrated at Duple Northern in Blackpool, which was to be re-named Duple Coachbuilders Limited. The Blackpool factory was based on the business of H. V. Burlingham Ltd. (who were best known for the Seagull body of the 1950s), which Duple had taken over in August 1960. In 1966 the company introduced the Viceroy range to replace the Bella series on most Bedford and Ford chassis! The second design, the Dominant, initially intended for a 1970 release, was beset by problems including an uncertain market, and it did not appear until 1972, and was thus too late to clothe the VAL70.

Top Right: *The later style of the Vega Major design inherited the original body structure, as will be seen by the continual use of the diagonal window pillar. The side trim however was given a broad band of colour and a thin bright strip to give a long horizontal look on the lower parallel; with quite large circular flashing indicators looking a little like an after thought. This 1966 coach (CCU 277D) was the second of four VAL14s that were purchased by Hall Bros of South Shields.*

Middle Right: *The frontal styling of the coach was later carried over to the early Viceroy design with different side trim. This was the Viceroy 36 (36') body on a VAL70 chassis supplied to Hunter of Loanhead in July 1968.*

Bottom Right: *Hendon was closed in 1970 and all production moved north, as Duple's output fell to just over 400 bodies; whilst at the same time Plaxton had seen its production rise to over 1,000 bodies in the same year. In 1971, the loss-making Willowbrook was separated and sold off. This Viceroy 37 (37') body had the new style front end on VAL70 (PDL 823H), which was new to Seaview Services on the Isle of Wight, but later went to the island's Regent Coaches.*

THE VAL 70

During the late-autumn of 1967 Vauxhall Motors announced the introduction of the Bedford VAL70 chassis, which was designed (as the name implied) for the forthcoming new decade. The first of these vehicles were displayed at that year's Scottish Commercial Vehicle Show in the Kelvin Hall, Glasgow. The new version of the VAL was actually a development of the previous model, designed for the fitting of a new Bedford 466 diesel engine, which had a capacity of 7.63-litres.

Yet, this was only the first step in even more fundamental changes that would come in the Bedford coach chassis range, and by the time of its introduction further development of the VAM had appeared, whilst a new underfloor engined Bedford chassis was already undergoing tests.

Above: *Appearing at the 1968 Commercial Motor Show was this example of the VAL 70, fitted with the latest in designs of luxury coachwork from Plaxton, the Panorama Elite. It displayed the fictional registration plate PLA 69, (Plaxton 1969) but became NED 537G in the Barry Cooper fleet at Warrington.* Plaxton

Accordingly, 'the writing was on the wall' for the novel twin-steer chassis, as the Construction & Use regulations were due for a further update, and major changes in the industry were envisaged as a result of the forthcoming Transport Act of 1968. There was no immediate intention to stop a 'good thing' when it was still selling well, and the increasing size of the motorway network meant there were plenty of VAL orders coming in. Yet the Dunstable plant was planning for a new generation of PSV.

Originally, the VAL14 chassis number had consisted of four digits, but this was changed in 1966 to a figure reading 68, followed by a five digit number. This was again changed the following year when the first two numbers were 78. Later in 1967 the chassis number changed to 7T, which was followed by six digits. The chassis numbering sequence then changed yearly until 1972 when the last of the VAL 70 chassis, completed in 1973, carried 2T474319.

This coach was fitted with a Panorama Elite coach body. and supplied to Danby of Hull in April 1973 as GAT 502L. This however does not suggest that this coach was the last one to enter service, for as with all bus and coach manufacturers the chassis production facilities were always ahead of body production and there were at least three more VAL coaches that entered service two months after this vehicle. Some of the more significant VAL70 owners included a raft of firms in Cheshire, including the Jacksons-Pleasureways-Shearings combine, whilst Bostocks of Congleton also continued their association with the Marque.

Meanwhile, Shaw of Coventry took five (SHP 761-5G), another big order was from Rendell of Parkstone who had six (MPR 531-6H), whilst Guards of London went one better with seven Plaxton-bodied coaches (TAR 183-9J). The last multiple order was for three April 1973 VAL70s, which were supplied to Exclusive of Hounslow (RBY 42-4L).

However, the striking thing about the sale register for the VAL70, is the large number of small independent buyers that formed the core customer base; most having only a solitary VAL in their fleet. Vauxhall had to change this position with its next generation of coaches, recognising that they had to produce a model that would appeal to the economics of the newly nationalised part of the British bus industry.

Top Right: *Wearing the more simple lines of the Panorama Elite, this VAL 70 was supplied to Southern Vectis, which by then had surrendered its well know livery for the National overall white with red and blue lettering and insignia.*

Middle Right: *Among the pristine coaches that were taking part in the 16th British Coach Rally at Brighton was this Plaxton bodied coach of Tatlock's. Like many of Tatlock's coaches MEN 329H was named, this one again being* Edith.

Bottom Right: *Carrying the new Elite body CAR 433K was new to Perth Coaches and was photographed along Brighton Esplanade whilst taking part in the 18th British Coach Rally.*

Above: *A newcomer to the British scene is illustrated here with Caetano Estoril coachwork with seating for 53 passengers for Grayline of Bicester. Note the distinctive paint scheme on VAL70 chassis (TBW 718G), which although 'tame' by today's schemes was quite a culture shock in the 1960s.*

During the time that the VAL70 appeared, one or two European coachbuilders considered chancing their arm on the British market as well. Some of these were new to the Bedford Marque, although they had commonly bodied other chassis from General Motors (Vauxhall-Bedford's parent company), whilst builders like the Dutch firm Van Hool had long enjoyed a good association with Bedford products.

Perhaps the most successful of these new boys was the Portuguese Caetano company, who operated through a British agency named Alfred Moseley of Loughborough in order to gain orders and handle distribution. It was in 1946 that the seed of the Caetano company was sown, when the firm of Martins Caetano & Irmao was established, building wooden-framed coach and bus bodies.

Salvador Caetano was never slow to move with the times, and in 1952 he was the first coach builder in Portugal to use the composite (wood/steel) framing for coach bodies. They followed this in 1955, when they began building buses of all-steel construction. In 1965, the firm opened a new factory at Oliveira do Douro and then found itself with the capacity to serve more than just Portuguese demand. Consequently, the export potential was investigated and the first of these new 'sectors' became the UK coach market in 1967.

Caetano went on to body a score of VAL70 chassis with their Estoril design, which was named after a popular holiday destination near Lisbon. Lisbon also gave its name to another of the Caetano designs, the Lisboa, which were supplied for various other chassis such as the Bedford VAM. It is thought that the first of the Caetano Estoril-bodied VAL coaches was supplied to Stanley Gath, a small tour operator that was based near Dewsbury in West Yorkshire. That coach, registered FHD 856G (chassis 9T463642) was supplied in March 1969, the last Estoril-VALs were delivered to Hambridge of Kidlington and Mills of Gornal Wood in May 1971.

Contrasting from the curvaceous designs that were usual on European coaches during the previous decades. The Caetano design followed the rather boxy style of European practice that was then in vogue. Of its curiously-shaped side windows above the leading axles, a Duple salesman of the time is reputed to say that the design was just a Vega Major body put on backwards! The radiator grille was also rather a fussy affair, although in a quite stylish sense.

The majority of the Caetano bodies appear to have been finished in liveries that utilised a multitude of stripes of various lengths and thicknesses; a foretaste of things to come on a large number of coaches on British roads during the following decades. However, and whether or not this was significant, only one British concern purchased more than a solitary example. This was Western Roadways of Patchway, who took four into stock during 1969. these were registered RDF 878-881G, and like the majority of these bodies were 53-seater coaches. The 16 other examples of the Caetano Estoril that were sold in this country were delivered to various independent concerns the length and breadth of the land.

Top Right: *The registration on this VAL70 was not a private plate, but stands for Alf Moseley 1970, and this coach became FDH 807H. The Portuguese bodies were marketed in this country by the Moseley group as the Moseley Continental. The coach carrying the Walsall Football Club name on the illuminated side panel was built on the Bedford VAM chassis and fitted with the Caetano Cascais style of coachwork. This view was taken at Mosley's Shepshed showrooms at the October Show in 1969.* Vauxhall Motors

Middle Right: *Caetano of Portugal enjoyed an excellent reputation in Portugal, and during 1967 they made their first tentative moves into Britain. Quite why the UK market opened up so readily to foreign competition is a matter of debate, but within a decade both British-made bodies and PSV chassis were facing stiff European competition. Bendelow & Sons purchased this VAL70/Estoril coach (UYC 799G), which had been new to R & S of London W8 in March 1969.*

Bottom Right: *Eddie Brown of Helperby, Yorkshire was also a coach operator who liked the Continental styles. Their 1969 example of a VAL 70 with a Caetano Estoril body was registered PPY 551G and is seen here while on hire to the West Yorkshire Road Car Company for a tour to Scarborough, where it would drive past the Plaxton factory.*

Above: *This was without doubt the rarest of all of the Bedford VAL coaches that were constructed for a British based psv operator. Indeed, Van Hool only bodied two VAL70s, RAR 690J shown here and KNT 1, which was a mobile display unit for the Kent Group and thus a non-PSV. At the time of this picture, RAR 690J was with Magulls Coaches of Liverpool, but was new to All Seasons of London W2. Robert Franklin*

A handful of the other European coachbuilders also created very commendable designs of coachwork for the Bedford VAL chassis but in the main those were built onto chassis that were exported. One exception however was the VAL 70 chassis that was given the registration number RAR 690J, and was the first major attempt by the Dutch builder to break into the Bedford coach market in the UK.

As noted in *Bedford Buses of the 1950s & '60s*, Van Hool began bodying the OB for operators in the Low Countries not long after it was re-introduced there in the second half of the 1940s. They also built a range of bodies on the SB, and allegedly one or two on export VAL14 chassis. However, their first for the UK market was built on chassis number 1T461819, and this was followed by a second model for use as a mobile showroom (KNT 1). The coach was a rather boxy affair, with the cabin area fashioned to look a little lower than the seating area. The cabin area was then finished with two shallow, curved windows in the roof set a little further back than the actual front profile giving the cabin area a stepped down appearance. The design was called the 'Vista Dome' on account of this. The 51-seater Van Hool coach was delivered new in January 1971 to 'All Seasons' of London W2.

There were various other European coachbuilders such as Jonckheere, Soro, and Stollen that created bodies for fitting to Bedford VAL chassis but these were all fitted to the chassis that were exported to Europe. If any reader can help trace the export VAL models, we would be interested in featuring an article on these in our sister magazine *Vintage Roadscene*. Van Hool and Caetano, continue to create many coach bodies for other British PSV chassis, and in doing so paved the way for the position of European builders in the modern British coaching market.

When it comes to the bodies shipped to the Indian subcontinent, Austral-Asia, South Africa, and the Middle East, the position is entirely one of *ad-hoc* confusion. Seemingly credible information from one source, later being disproved by another. None of this is helped by the fact that the Export Sales register, whilst still in existence, has not been available for inspection. Sadly, these records, like several other Bedford archive files, were retained 'in lieu of wages' by employees of what remained of the Bedford Truck & Bus Plant, when they failed to get paid by AWD who took over the vestiges of the firm after General Motors decided to cease truck and bus building in Britain.

The dissipation of valuable archive material has left a number of blanks in the records for the British market as well, and it can only be hoped that these items will all be brought back together under one roof in the future. Logically, the best place for these would be in the Vauxhall Heritage Centre archives at Luton, but sadly (in common with many modern car producers), the heritage aspects of the business do not always figure high on the list of priorities. Perhaps the organisers of the Bedford Owners Club or the Bedford Gathering event might therefore one day become a more appropriate repository. Both organisations have excellent internet web-sites, and readers are recommended to visit these for details of what services they have to offer.

Below: This VAL14 coach proved that the proud exclamation of the Bedford "You see them everywhere", was no idle boast. Even the VAL chassis travelled to the far side of the world ! For instance, this coach of Days Motors Ltd is seen in Christchurch, New Zealand. It was used predominantly for sightseeing tours and was finished with a local built 'Midland' body to full luxury coach specification. Vauxhall Motors

COME FLY WITH ME

The majority of British passenger airlines found it expedient to operate their own fleet of buses and coaches. These were used for the transfer of passengers and luggage to and from the airport terminals to the plane, and never went on the public highways; meaning that they were un-registered. Others provided a scheduled service from an airport to a nearby city centre, and these naturally carried registration plates. Bedford supplied a few bus chassis for these duties over the years, as can be seen from the first two books in this series, but they were not unique. For instance, many of their competitors will come readily to mind, including the half-deck Commer Commando's or the front entrance AEC Routemaster with luggage trailers that were owned by BEA, or indeed the many and varied BOAC coaches in their blue and white livery; not least the ones that appeared in Dinky Toy model form.

Above: *The very popular Duple Viceroy was built in both 36' and 37' lengths. Shannon Greyhound had some smartly attired and attractive cabin crew and this promotional example of the Bedford VAL (JCU 370G) for airport duties. This coach was later re-registered as FZU 875 and JCU 370G went on to a Bedford VAM70/Duple Viceroy coach.* Vauxhall Motors

Many airline utilised luxury coaches, such as the body types built by Plaxton and Duple on various chassis. While certain cities in Britain also had airport buses within their municipal bus fleets. Manchester used a dual blue livery for their buses that served Manchester airport to distinguish them from the normal bus service fleet. Liverpool, even operated four specially constructed vehicles, for a service between Lime Street Station and Speke Airport, these were Leyland Royal Tigers PSU1/13 with Metro-Cammell half-deck bodies, but their fleet had earlier included both OB and SB Bedford models.

As we have mentioned the type and style of vehicles chosen by various airlines for this line of work varied enormously. During the mid 1960s the British Overseas Airways Corporation, (BOAC) had a fleet of Ford coaches with Duple 43 seat 'Marauder' bodies. However around that time the company had used some 'Standerwick' Leyland Atlantean double deck coaches for trials. The results of that exercise led to BOAC placing an order for 15 Leyland Atlanteans with Metro-Cammell H38/16F bodies. The vehicles were fitted with coach seats and incorporated generous luggage accommodation too.

With the introduction of the VAL chassis in 1962, one of the Duple demonstrators was sent to the Irish Republic, and whilst there it spent some time working with Aer Lingus at Shannon International Airport. It was found to be an excellent vehicle, and eventually a production VAL would be purchased for use at the airport. However, it was obvious that a better body would be needed if the VAL was to be used on internal airport transfers.

Consequently, Vauxhall approached Marshalls of Cambridge in 1964 with a view to their constructing an airport demonstrator on a VAL14 chassis. They allocated a chassis (allegedly 1768) for the purpose, and this was given a dual door 48-seat body and loaned to BEA at Ruislip for evaluation. It was later returned to Cambridge and the centre door sealed up and turned into a 52-seater, Whether this became the vehicle that was sold to Burton of Brixham in June 1965 is not known, but the picture of that vehicle shown on page 17 does have a rather distorted look in the lower body panels that are situated in between the front and rear wheels.

Below: *Trans-World Airlines (TWA) acquired a small fleet of VAL14 buses for Heathrow Airport. These had been built by Marshall of Cambridge and were unusual in having twin sliding passenger doors on both sides of the buses, as seen on the first one in this line up (RAR 269D). Vauxhall Motors*

Above: *Very similar in appearance to the TWA airport buses that were illustrated on the previous page, the earlier LMG 156C was a 1965 member of the first batch operated by BEA at Heathrow on transfer duties.* Vauxhall Motors

Whatever the case with the original demonstrator, BEA were suitably impressed to place an order for ten VAL14s with Marshall 40-seat bodywork in July 1965. These were delivered to the Northolt Depot of BEA in October and November that year as LMG 155-64C. Manchester City Transport liked the idea and tested a Plaxton-bodied VAL14, before ordering three in 1966 for the Manchester Piccadilly - Ringway Airport service, followed by five more in 1968 and two in May 1969.

BEA went back to Marshall for another pair in 1967 (OGO 337/40E) and eight more in 1967 (OYF 262-9F). Also in 1966, Interline of WC2 took four 40-seat Marshall-bodied coaches for airline duties at Heathrow with TWA, using bodies very similar to those used on the BEA batch.

The Bedford VAL buses that were bodied by Marshall of Cambridge were of a unique design, utilising several components from various other designs, such as the Camagna and Cambrette, that Marshall were constructing at that time.

Marshall constructed these airport buses on the conventional right-hand drive Bedford VAL chassis with an off-side driver's door. However, passenger access was not provided by an entrance ahead of the front axles as on the more normal designs of body from other coachbuilders. On the contrary, these buses were designed and constructed with twin entrance doors, centrally positioned, on either side of the vehicle and of an external sliding nature. Front and rear roof domes were peaked and similar in design to the style fitted to production fare-stage saloons that Marshall were constructing at that time. The front windscreen however was not of the double curvature but was an angled design as used in the Marshall Cambrette model. Finally, four cant-rail roof lights were provided to allow visibility of aircraft taking off and landing.

The construction of the back end incorporated three rear windows, including one in the central emergency door. At the front of the vehicle, the radiator grille was rather a plain unflattering construction, simple and quite business-like painted in the body colour. The roofs of these 'Airside Coaches' carried the obligatory flashing amber beacons. Internally, the Marshall-bodied Bedford VALs had all the seats arranged longitudinally, except for a rearward facing seat behind the driver. This arrangement allowed for a greater freedom of movement of passengers with hand luggage but also allowed for a high proportion of standing passengers too on the short run to the airport terminal.

A number of conventionally-bodied VAL14s and VAL70s served at airports or the roads leading to them, most of these were either Duple or Plaxton furnished chassis. They were not only used at British Airports, but also at overseas as well, including Shannon International and Johannesburg.

Top Right: *The illustration here gives a very clear insight to the interior of the Marshall bodied Bedford VAL airport buses that were operated by both BEA and TWA, although from the BEA coach seen through the VAL's windows on the left, this is probably a BEA example.. The perimeter seating does allow for easy movement for passengers boarding and alighting with hand luggage whilst the cantrail lights help to provide passengers with good visibility. Vauxhall Motors*

Middle Right: *The conventional Bedford VAL touring coach was also used by several airline companies in its more massed produced form. This VAL14 with Plaxton Panorama I body (GMB 112C) was serving with the British European Airways (BEA) Fleet. The reader will notice the small marker lights and the obligatory amber flashing roof beacons, Naturally, these would not have been fitted when the vehicle was a new coach to Shearings of Altrincham in January 1965,*

Bottom Right: *Somewhat overshadowed by the very large McAlpine name on the hanger in the distance, and the massive Lockheed Super Constellation aircraft of the Euravia Airline. The small fleet of seven VAL14 coaches, all of which are illustrated here, offered more refinement for the Sky Tours patrons than would normally be found on the more basic airport buses - the idea being that 'the holiday starts before you arrive'. These Duple Vega Major-bodied coaches (31 KNM and AXD 525-30B), were actually owned by Seamark and operated at Luton Airport. Vauxhall Motors*

THE CHESTER ENGINEERIN

CURIOUS CONTENDERS

Although the Bedford VAL was designed and built primarily for the PSV industry, the chassis was put to use in other applications. This became particularly evident with examples that had reached the second-hand market or were considered as time expired for touring duties, as their level, low-floor height made them ideal for other uses, especially racing car transporters and caravans.

In this chapter we will examine some of the curious contenders that used new VAL chassis for other purposes. Although there are widely different figures quoted for export VALs and the non-PSV applications, it still seems impossible to unravel the precise number. The previous book on the VAL chassis, entitled *Twin Steer,* states that at least 42 were exported as overseas PSVs, of which 24 were left-hand-drive. However, information has subsequently come to light of VALs being used in countries not listed in that publication.

Above: *One of the more unusual VAL14s, was this transporter built by Cheshire Engineering. Unlike its fellows, chassis 1860 (FFM 105C) was not destined to take patrons on their holidays, but built to take their holiday home to them. This was actually the first VAL chassis that was bodied from new as a non-PSV application passenger in 1965. Vauxhall Motors*

The first non-PSV VAL turned out to be the experimental chassis RHD62/1, which was stripped of its MCW Topaz body and reclaimed by Vauxhall for their own promotional use. No progress was made with the use of the racing car transporter that was made from an amalgam of the chassis and the experimental Plaxton VAL body, but during 1965 it became clear to Bedford managers why this was. Unknown to even the senior people at Dunstable, the HQ at Luton had done a deal with the motor racing star, Jack (later Sir Jack) Brabham, whereby he would lend his name to Vauxhall in order to promote their car range, notably a sports version of the new HB Viva.

As part of the deal, it was decided to make the would-be Vauxhall Racing Transporter available to the Brabham Racing Organisation, who by that time had taken on the aforementioned Denny Hulme as their Number Two driver; thus replacing Dan Gurney who had left Brabham to pursue other Formula One and racing interests. The transporter was handed over for the 1966 season, and whilst it did not take part in any races, it played a major part in what was a remarkable team success story. By 1966 the cars were Brabham-Repco, with the Australian Repco company providing tremendous support and building the Formula One engines. The combination took Brabham to his third F1 World Driver's Championship in 1966, and this feat was followed by Hulme in 1967.

The first non-PSV use of a production VAL chassis was with 1860 in May 1965, which was bodied by Cheshire Engineering Ltd. as a caravan transporter. It was used for many years delivering Sprite Caravans from Crabtree Caravans Ltd. of Northwich, Cheshire. It is said that the caravan company got the idea of using the VAL from the coaching company of Bostocks in nearby Congleton, who themselves were well taken with the VAL after getting early chassis 1076 (776 LG) whilst 1077 (7 KX) had gone to Todd of Whitchurch after a local Bedford sales agent, Robert Lightowler, had actively toured the area with the Plaxton VAL/RHD62/1 demonstrator. Robert says that, if you look at the sales of the early VALs in Cheshire and the Welsh Marches, the records will show he earned his commission.

Top Right: *Although we used this picture in* Bedford Buses of the 1950s & '60s, *its importance in the VAL story means it could not be excluded from this publication. Note will be made of the lower floor height at the back, which meant that a simple pair of ramps allowed access. The transporter remained with Brabham for around 10-years.* Vauxhall Motors

Middle Right: *One of more unusual commercial vehicle applications for the Bedford VAL chassis was this German-bodied car transporter, which was used by a Belgium company to collect cars from Opel. Notice will be taken of the small diameter wheels of the VAL chassis, while those on the four-wheeled trailer are of a larger diameter.* Vauxhall Motors

Bottom Right: *Van Hool bodies were not common sights on VAL chassis here in Britain, although several were made for Europe. However, a real hybrid is this left-hand-drive VAL70 with a Van Hool body, which was made for the George Kent Group as a mobile showroom.* John L. Kaye

Above: *In the 1930s, the London & North Eastern and Southern railways puchased Maudslay bus chassis for use as horseboxes. This VAL70 (GNR 844L) continues the tradition with a G. C. Smith body.* Historic Commercial Vehicle Society

Left: *This VAL was the second pigeon transporter purchased by Chris Catterall of Hambleton in Lancashire. The vehicle was fitted with a Plaxton front end, but we are unsure which coachbuilder bodied this VAL70 (KTE 328F) or Catterall's earlier VAL1414 (CTE 688E); it has been suggested that this may have been a product by Cockers.* Vauxhall Motors

Right: *Here we see the very unusual Dell-bodied Bedford VAL70 (OOW 999G) in its pristine two-tone blue and white livery of Southern Television.* Paul Marshall

Other commercial applications of the VAL chassis included horseboxes, and it has long been acknowledged that at least three examples were constructed; these being VAL14 GOU 764D by Lambourn, VAL70s DDP 828K and GNR 844L, by Vincent and G. C. Smith respectively. However, we are reliably informed that Smith's built at least two VAL horseboxes for the UK, and one for Germany, which carried an Opel badge. They also supplied a new horsebox body on a second-hand VAL14 chassis, which was made for an owner near Thirsk.

In 1966, a VAL14 (18 RN 22) was ordered by the Royal Navy for a Mass Radiography Unit at HM Dockyard Portsmouth. In light of this, the National Health Service considered ordering 12 VAL14 chassis for similar units in order to replace its aging fleet of Leyland Beaver lorries and trailer units that were used for radiography duties on a regional basis. A VAL14 demonstrator was sent to Adams & Gibbons, a Newcastle-based Bedford dealer, in order for the NHS to do driver evaluation at the city's Royal Victoria Infirmary. Favourable reports were received and an order for 12 was confirmed, along with a further 12 VAL 14s for the regional Blood Transfusion units.

However, Bedford was then phasing out the VAL14 chassis in favour of the VAL70 and they offered these as an alternative! This offer was not accepted by the NHS, primarily on account of the higher cost of the newer chassis. Nevertheless, the Navy ordered a second Mass Radiograph Unit (13 RN 11), a VAL70 that was run alongside the earlier model for around 12-months prior to the VAL14 being disposed of.

Among the other applications that VAL chassis were put to in non-PSV roles included those built as outside broadcast units for independent television. These were GNF 951E and HXJ 846F, both VAL14s with bodies by Road Transport Services for Granada TV. A third example was Southern TV's VAL70 (OOW 999G). This has now been restored to full working condition by its present owner, Paul Marshall of Newark who is a Marconi electronics engineer.

A number of BBC Outside Broadcast vehicles of the 1960s have often been described as on VAL chassis, as they too employed the twin-steer arrangement. These were however Eagle-bodied units, on other chassis types that were fitted with an extra Primrose axle at the front.

Another VAL70 to work in the film world was GLF 325J, which carried a Swiss-built body for Filmstrasse AG of Zurich! The National Coal Board also had a VAL as a mobile film unit, but few details are known about (JOW 951E), other than it was bodied by a Southampton bodybuilder (probably Sparshatt); this may have originally been owned by Southern TV and thus a precursor to OOW 999G. Others have said that it may have been GNF 951E, but that vehicle was still in Granada's ownership when the NCB are reported to have obtained their unit.

We should next consider the VALs that were load carriers. Several Pantechnicon bodies were produced, including KJU 797E with a Crawford body, three Marsden-bodied VAL70s (TED 125H, UED 108J and YED 661K), which were made for Sharnware Manufacturing, whilst more Marsden van bodies were produced for VAL70s KMP 111K and UWR 144L. Abrams bodied VXJ 397-8L, and G C Smith's produced at least three pantechnicons, one of which was HNR 455L.

Below: *Seen at the Sparshatt works prior to delivery and registration, this VAL70 would become CGU 78H for the Road Transport Industry Training Board and based at High Ercall in Shropshire.* Historic Commercial Vehicle Society

Other applications saw a Sparshatt mobile classroom body on the Road Transport Industry Training Board's CGU 78H, and PSG 858H (Duple) and KNT 1 (a left-hand drive chassis with a Van Hool body) that both became mobile showrooms. But surely the award for the most extravagantly built Bedford VAL must go to VMO 770H. That vehicle was not only built with a special body, but given a fourth (rear) axle by York Trailers.

Finally, we must mention the batch of VALs that were converted for use as medical transports, a role for which they were ideal due to their low-floor height and thus ease of wheelchair access. These included at least one VAL for the Red Cross (believed to have been sent to the Middle East in 1967, Then came VAL70 RJE 414J, with an Appleyard/Smiths of Gateshead 38-seat body for a Cambridgeshire hospital; YSN 10K, a Scottish Motor Traction 16-seat body for Kirkintilloch; a second SMT-bodied example (CWG 753L) went to the Central Regional Council; and finally, what is believed to have been the G C Smith-bodied LBD 529L for Northamptonshire Health Authority in 1973.

Of course, due to their low-floor level chassis, many VAL PSVs saw second lives after they were converted for other uses, including caravans, car transporters, horseboxes.

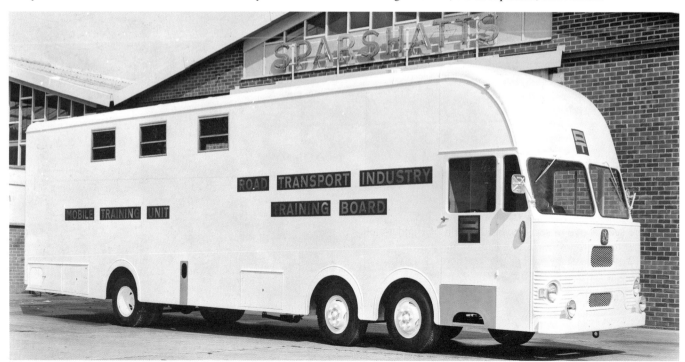

THEY WHO ALSO SERVED

Throughout the 11-year run of the VAL and long after it ended, the SB coach chassis that it was intended to replace remained in production. Despite the advent of the mid-range VAM and the smaller 29-seat VAS, the SB continued to sell well. Ranging from the early Plaxton-bodied model (a pair of which are seen above in service with Hanson of Huddersfield - well I had to get this firm in one way or another), to the later models like the Plaxton Elite-bodied coach to the right.

The reason for including these vehicles at the end of a book on the Bedford VAL, is that the SB will form the next episode in the Bedford Buses series. If you have any memories or photographs of the Bedford SB that you would like to contribute towards this publication, please contact the author at the publisher's Appleby address shown on page 2 of this book.

ACKNOWLEDGEMENTS

This book could not possibly have come together without the help and encouragement of the following people, many of whom contributed photographs, while others helped in more technical ways, and I would like to record my sincere thanks to all the people involved during the six years that this book has been researched, including: Peter Blincow John Bristow, Shane Conway, Alan & Larraine Earnshaw, Martin Dickinson, Martin Eltham, Robert Franklin, Tony J. Griffin, Dave Haddock, Richard Haughey David Heywood, John Hood, John Kaye, Malcolm Knight, John Locke, Walter Lord, Paul Marshall, Alan Miller, Matthew Richardson, Dave Sayer, Dennis Sherer, S.W. Stevens-Stratten, Chris Taylor, Ted Taylor, Theo Taylor, David Townend, Andrew Webster and Malcolm Wright.

Above: *This VAL 70 enjoys a day out in the North-West sunshine while competing in the driving test as entrant number 53 at the Blackpool Coach Rally. The vehicle was in pristine condition, even the wheel-arches are immaculately clean. Plaxton Panorama Elite II coachwork was the style chosen by Bostocks of Congleton for FLG 360K, which was allocated fleet number 19 when acquired in 1972.*

I must also thank the following companies and organisations: Vauxhall Motors, The Bedford Gathering Team, The Bedford Owners Club, Plaxton, Duple Motor Bodies Ltd., The Historic Commercial Vehicle Society, the Manchester Museum of Transport, and the PSV Circle. I must also thank the support of a wide cross-section of people, including many enthusiasts and professionals in the bus and coach industry,